SCIENCE PROJECTS

ELECTRICITY

Simon de Pinna

Photography by

Chris Fairclough

HODDER
Wayland

an imprint of Hodder Children's Books

Produced for Hodder Wayland by
The Creative Publishing Company
Unit 3, 37 Watling Street, Leintwardine
Shropshire SY7 0LW, England

First published in Great Britain in 1997
by Wayland (Publishers) Ltd

Reprinted in 2000 by Hodder Wayland,
an imprint of Hodder Children's Books

Hodder Children's Books
A division of Hodder Headline Ltd
338 Euston Road
London NW1 3BH

British Library Cataloguing in Publication Data
De Pinna, Simon
  Electricity (Science Projects)
  1. Electricity – Juvenile literature 2. Electricity –
Experiments – Juvenile literature
I. Title
537

ISBN 0 7502 3396 6

Printed and bound in Italy by
G. Canale & C.S.p.A., Turin

Commissioned photography: Chris Fairclough
Consultant: Jeremy Bloomfield
Designer: Ian Winton
Illustrations: Julian Baker

Picture acknowledgements
The publishers would like to thank the following
for permission to reproduce their pictures:

Science Photo Library: front cover (Jeremy
Burgess), pages 6 (Peter Menzel), 22 (US
Department of Energy), 36 (Martin Bond), 38 (Alex
Bartel); **Tony Stone Images:** pages 4 (Doug
Armand), 8 (Andy Sachs), 19 (Patrick Ingrand), 26
(Bruce Forster), 28 (Dennis O'Clair), 44 (Bruce
Forster).

The publishers would like to thank the staff and
pupils of Harborne Junior School, Birmingham,
for their help in the preparation of this book.

The publishers also wish to thank Philip Harris
Education for kindly loaning various materials used
in the projects in this volume.

NATIONAL CURRICULUM NOTES

The investigations in this book are cross-referenced to Programmes of Study for Science at
Key Stages 2, 3 and 4.

STATIC ELECTRICITY, USING STATIC AND LIGHTNING
KS2 Sc3, 1c; KS3 Sc3, 1k; KS3 Sc4 (double) 1a & 1b; KS4
(double) Sc3, 1c & 1e; KS4 (double) Sc4, 1k, 1n & 1o
CELLS AND BATTERIES KS3 Sc4, 1b, 1f & 5f; KS4 (double) Sc3,
1b, 1c & 1e; KS4 (double) Sc4, 1b & 1q; KS4 (single) Sc3, 1b
MAKING CIRCUITS KS2 Sc4, 1a; KS3 Sc4, 1e
TURN IT ON KS2 Sc4, 1b
SERIES AND PARALLEL KS2 Sc4, 1c; KS3 Sc4, 1d; KS4
(double) Sc4, 1a; KS4 (single) Sc4, 1a
CIRCUIT DIAGRAMS KS2 Sc4, 1d
CONDUCTIVITY KS2 Sc3, 1c; KS3 Sc3, 1j & 1k
RESISTANCE KS2 Sc3, 1c; KS3 Sc3, 1j & 1k; KS3 Sc4, 1d; KS4
(double) Sc4, 1d & 1f; KS4 (single) Sc4, 1d & 1f
PRODUCING HEAT KS3 Sc3, 1j; KS3 Sc4, 5f; KS4 (double)
Sc4, 1c, 1i & 1l; KS4 (single) Sc4, 1c, 1f & 1j

ELECTRIC LIGHT KS3 Sc3, 1j; KS3 Sc4, 5f; KS4 (double)
Sc4, 1c, 1i & 1l; KS4 (single) Sc4, 1c, 1f & 1j
ELECTROLYSIS and **ELECTROPLATING** KS2 Sc3, 1c; KS3
Sc3, 1j; KS4 (double) Sc3, 1i & 2l; KS4 (double) Sc4, 1q
ELECTROMAGNETISM KS3 Sc4, 1g, 1i & 1j; KS4 (double)
Sc4, 1s; KS4 (single) Sc4, 1l
ELECTRIC MOTORS KS3 Sc4, 1g, 1i & 1j; KS4 (double)
Sc4, 1s; KS4 (single) Sc4, 1l
GENERATORS KS3 Sc4, 5c & 5f; KS4 (double) Sc4, 1j, 1m,
1t, 1u & 1w; KS4 (single)
ELECTRICITY SUPPLY KS3 Sc4, 5c & 5f; KS4 (double) Sc4,
1j, 1m, 1t, 1u & 1w; KS4 (single) Sc4, 1h, 1k, 1m & 1n
KEEPING SAFE KS4 (double) Sc4, 1k; KS4 (single) Sc4, 1i
ELECTRONICS KS2 Sc4, 1b; KS4 (double) Sc4, 1g; KS4
(single) Sc4, 1g

CONTENTS

ELECTRICITY AT WORK

Nearly everywhere you go, you will find electricity at work. Over the last one hundred years, it has completely changed people's lives. Devices powered by electricity make our lives comfortable and provide entertainment at home, at school and in the places where we work.

Electricity is relatively easy to make and send to where it is needed. It can be changed into other forms of energy, such as light and heat. A telephone changes sound into electricity and vice versa, while an electric fan converts electricity into the movement of blades to cool you down, and an electric kettle turns electrical energy into heat.

Thousands of electric lights shine brilliantly at the Oktoberfest in Berlin.

Outside the home, too, electricity is in constant demand – in hospitals, for example, to keep working the machines that maintain life during operations.

The sort of electricity we use whenever we plug in a machine at a wall socket is called current electricity. The other kind of electricity is called static electricity. You can make this kind for yourself, but it isn't as useful as current electricity. Static electricity produces the lightning you see during a thunderstorm and makes your hair stand on end when you comb it.

MY ELECTRIC LIFE

1. Make three lists in your notebook:
List 1: the electrical objects that you use every day at home or at school.
List 2: other electrical things that you use from time to time.
List 3: any other examples of electricity in action outside the home.

2. Make a poster to show all the objects you have listed. Put your name or your photo at the centre of the poster.

3. Sketch or cut out pictures of the things in List 1 and stick them to the left of your name or photo.

4. To the right stick pictures in List 2.

5. Stick pictures in List 3 all around the edge of the poster.

6. Talk about your poster with a friend or someone in your family. Ask a friend to choose one thing from your List 1, which you should agree not to use for one week. After one week, discuss with your friend how your life changed without that object. What did you do instead? Did you find something else electrical to take its place? Would your friend's choices be similar or very different?

MATERIALS

- a notebook
- coloured pens and pencils
- used magazines and catalogues of electrical objects
- a poster-size sheet of coloured paper
- glue
- scissors

Did you know?

The English physicist Michael Faraday showed in 1831 how electricity could be made, but it wasn't until the 1870s that electricity was used to light streets and public buildings. The first attempt to supply electricity to people's homes was made in 1881, in the English town of Godalming.

STATIC ELECTRICITY

The crackling sound you sometimes hear when you pull off a sweater is caused by static electricity. If you take off your clothes in the dark, you can sometimes see sparks jumping from them. After you've been on a long car journey, you may feel an electric shock when you touch a metal doorknob. Again, these effects happen because of static electricity.

All substances are made up of atoms that have a nucleus at the centre and much smaller particles called electrons moving around the outside. There is a force that stops electrons moving away from the nucleus – this force is due to the particles in the atom having what is called electric charge. The nucleus of the atom has a positive electric charge and the electrons have a negative charge. Positive and negative charges attract each other so they tend to stay close together. However, negatively charged

A Van de Graaf generator produces large amounts of electric charge. A moving belt carries the charge up to a metal dome, where it builds up. Some of these generators can produce huge sparks when they lose their charge. They can even make your hair stand on end!

POSITIVE AND NEGATIVE

1. Suspend the plastic bottle from the string and rub it with the cotton cloth or handkerchief.

2. Rub the plastic pen with the cloth and bring the pen close to the bottle. Observe what happens. Can you explain what you see in terms of positive and negative electric charges?

3. Repeat steps **1** and **2**, but use a glass bottle instead of plastic. Again, observe what happens and explain what you see in terms of electric charges.

MATERIALS
- a plastic bottle
- a glass bottle
- a piece of string
- a cotton cloth or handkerchief
- a plastic pen

electrons repel each other, so they tend to be spaced out fairly evenly in any material. In most substances, except for metals, atoms hold their electrons firmly in orbit. However, it is sometimes possible to remove the electrons held by atoms on the surface of a non-metallic substance.

If you rub a plastic comb with a duster, electrons jump from the atoms on the surface of the duster to spread out on the surface of the comb. This gives the comb an excess of electrons and a negative electric charge. If you then bring the comb close to a pile of small pieces of paper, the extra electrons on the comb repel the electrons on the surface of the paper, leaving only the positively charged nuclei at the surface. Positive and negative charges attract each other, so the paper jumps up to the comb.

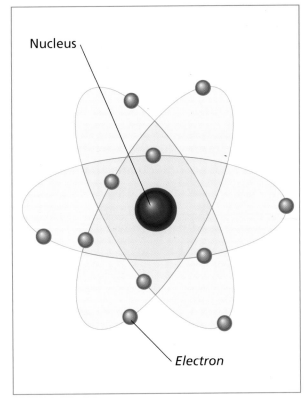

A simple model of an atom, but not to scale. For a nucleus this size, the electrons would be about ten metres away!

WATER BENDER

1. Pump up the balloon and tie a knot in the neck.

2. Rub the balloon against your sweater. After a small amount of rubbing, the balloon will carry a negative charge.

3. Hold the balloon near a stream of water. What happens to the water stream? Try not to let the balloon get wet, or the effect disappears. Why do you think that happens?

MATERIALS

● a balloon and pump

● a sweater

● a water tap

USING STATIC

If you tried the water-bending experiment on page 7, you will have noticed that the water stream curved towards the balloon. This was because negative charges on the surface of the balloon repelled electrons from the near side of the water and attracted the positively charged atomic nuclei. The process of forcing an object to become charged in this way is called electrostatic induction. Induction is put to use in several ways, from photocopying documents to dusting crops with pest-killing spray.

In a photocopier, a bright light creates an invisible image of the document on a large drum. This image is in the form of positively charged particles. In turn, these attract particles of a fine black powder, changing the invisible image to one that can be seen. This image is transferred to a sheet of paper as it passes around the drum. Finally, the toner is melted by a heated roller so that it sticks permanently to the paper.

A crop-spraying plane reduces the amount of pesticide chemical spray that is wasted by using electrostatic spray nozzles. Each of these contains a positively charged needle that takes electrons away from the droplets of spray, inducing a positive charge on their surfaces. When the droplets land on the leaves of plants, they are attracted towards the negatively charged electrons on the leaves. This attraction ensures that the leaves are evenly coated with chemical and very little blows away in the wind.

This crop of sweetcorn is being sprayed with pesticide by an aeroplane equipped with electrostatic spray nozzles.

SILLY SNAKES

1. Draw the outlines of 10 S-shapes on the paper. Cut them out and place them on the baking sheet. These are your 'snakes'.

MATERIALS

- a sheet of stiff paper
- scissors
- a pencil
- a metal baking sheet
- a balloon and pump
- a sweater

2. Blow up the balloon and tie a knot in the neck.

Did you know?

When a car is sprayed with paint, the paint droplets are given an electric charge to attract them to the car's body and give it an even coating.

3. Rub the balloon against the sweater to give it a negative charge.

4. Hold the balloon about 10 cm above your snakes and watch what happens. Can you explain what you see in terms of electrostatic induction?

LIGHTNING

Flashes of lightning occur when an electric charge builds up inside a cloud. Lightning is the discharge of electricity to the ground or to another cloud. The air around the lightning path becomes incredibly hot – up to 30,000°C – and it expands very quickly, causing shock waves that we hear as thunder. The brilliant flash of light you see when lightning flows from a cloud to the ground is called forked lightning. Sheet lightning is a glow that lights up the sky and is made when lightning flashes within the cloud itself.

Storms that involve lightning usually happen after a spell of hot weather, when a pocket of warm air rises rapidly through colder air. A thundercloud develops, with lighter, positively charged particles at the top and heavier, negatively charged water droplets at the bottom. These repel negatively charged particles in the ground below the cloud and so the ground gains a positive charge.

If the difference between the amounts of charge in the cloud and the ground is big enough, the cloud will discharge into the ground as a flash of lightning. The first stroke, or 'leader', travels to the ground by the fastest route, sometimes a tree. A huge current follows the same path back from the ground up to the cloud, creating a brilliant flash – the

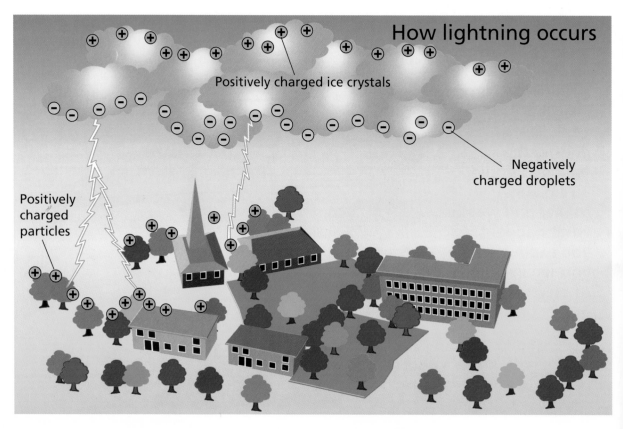

How lightning occurs

Positively charged ice crystals

Negatively charged droplets

Positively charged particles

'return' stroke – and an explosion – the clap of thunder. This sometimes seems to be happen well after the lightning, but that is only because light travels a thousand times faster than sound. More lightning strokes travel to the ground and back until the charges inside the cloud are balanced. This usually takes less than a second.

Did you know?

When lightning strikes, it chooses the path of least resistance, usually a high, pointed object. Many tall buildings have metal rods called lightning conductors attached to their uppermost points. Lightning will pass safely down the cable attached to the conductor and be neutralized by the earth.

STATIC DETECTOR

MATERIALS

- a glass jar
- kitchen foil
- a piece of stiff card
- a long nail
- cotton thread
- a plastic hairbrush or comb
- other objects to test for electricity, like a balloon, a pen, a pencil, or a ruler

1. Cut out a round card top for the glass jar, big enough to sit on the rim, and push the nail down through it.

2. Tie two short lengths of thread to the point of the nail and then tape two small squares of foil to them.

3. Tape the lid to the jar so that the pieces of foil hang down inside.

4. Rub the hairbrush or comb, or other plastic object, for at least a minute to charge it up. Hold the charged object on the head of the nail and observe what happens to the squares of foil. Can you explain what happens in terms of charges on the pieces of foil? The bigger the charge, the greater the effect on the foil.

5. If you grip the head of the nail, the charges run through you to earth and the foil pieces collapse. Investigate a range of charged objects and materials to see which can be charged up most.

CELLS AND BATTERIES

On page 6 you found out that all materials are made up of atoms, each of which is made up of a nucleus surrounded by negatively charged particles called electrons. The 1.5-volt batteries used in calculators, torches and personal stereos are properly called dry cells. Inside a dry cell is a paste made up of chemicals that react together to release 'spare' electrons at the negative end, or terminal, and produces a shortage of electrons at the other (positive) terminal. Larger batteries contain several cells joined together.

When a cell is connected into a circuit, the electrons at the negative terminal repel the electrons in the

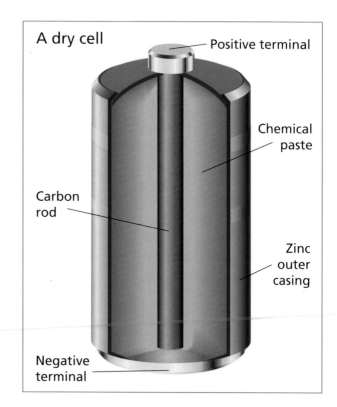

A dry cell

Positive terminal

Chemical paste

Carbon rod

Zinc outer casing

Negative terminal

FOOD CELLS

1. Push the large nail into the lemon and clip the bare end of one insulated wire to the head of the nail.

2. Attach the other end of the wire to a terminal of the bulb holder or clock module.

3. Attach the second wire to the brass screw and push it into the lemon.

4. Twist the other bare end of the wire around the other terminal of the bulbholder or clock module. Can you tell that an electric current is being made? You may need to black out the room to see any glow from the bulb.

MATERIALS

- a lemon and other juicy fruits
- a potato and other vegetables
- a large steel nail and a brass screw
- small pieces of other metals
- two lengths of insulated copper wire
- crocodile clips
- a 1.5-volt bulb and holder or a low-voltage digital clock module

wire. At the same time, the positive terminal of the battery attracts the electrons at the other end of the wire. The voltage of a cell or battery depends on the size of this force on the electrons. Its effect is to make loose electrons in the wire move towards the positive terminal, and the wave of moving electrons passing along the wire is the electric current.

Cars store electricity in a different sort of battery, called an accumulator. Accumulators consist of positive and negative lead plates surrounded by dilute acid. A car's battery supplies electricity for starting the car, keeping it running and working the lights, and can be recharged by the part of the car called the alternator, when the battery starts to go 'flat'.

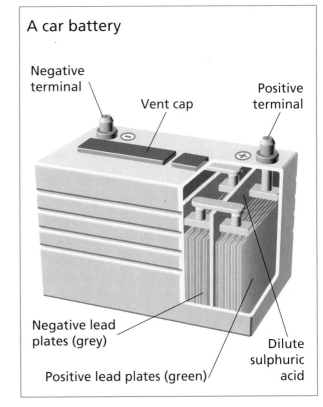

A car battery

Negative terminal

Vent cap

Positive terminal

Negative lead plates (grey)

Positive lead plates (green)

Dilute sulphuric acid

5. Try the experiment again with other fruits and vegetables, and using other pieces of metal instead of the screw.

6. Work out a way of telling which combination of metals and plant parts is the best for producing electricity.

MAKING CIRCUITS

When you turn on the switch to an electric light, electricity flows through a circle of wire called a circuit to light the bulb. What flows through the wire is called electric current and, if the circuit is broken, the current will not flow and the light will go out.

You can imagine electric current flowing around a circuit in a similar way to water being pumped through a pipe. Although you can't see the water flowing, you can see its effects by putting a small water wheel in the pipe. A light bulb in a circuit is like the water wheel: by lighting up, the bulb shows that current is flowing. Just as

the speed of the water wheel shows how much water is flowing past it, so the brightness of a bulb indicates how much current is going through it.

In the same way that the pump provides the energy to make the water flow through the pipe, the cell provides the energy to push electric current around the circuit. To keep flowing, the water must return to the pump and the electric current must return to the cell after it has travelled around the circuit. So, an electrical machine only works if it is connected by wires to both ends, or terminals, of the source of the electric current.

QUIZ CARDS

1. Write five sums on a sheet of card. Write the problems on the left and the answers on the right, but mix them up so that a problem is not next to its own answer. Leave a space of about 10 cm between the problems and the answers.

2. In the space, push two paper fasteners through the sheet of card so that they line up side-by-side between the first sum and first answer. Do the same for the other sums and answers.

MATERIALS
- ten paper fasteners
- a sheet of stiff card (20 cm x 15 cm)
- a reel of insulated wire
- crocodile clips
- two 1.5-volt cells and holders
- a bulb and holder
- a felt-tip pen

Did you know?
Printed circuits are found in many electrical machines. They are plastic boards with patterns of lines connecting different parts of the circuit. The lines show the path of electric current as it flows from one electronic component to the next – to make a calculation, perhaps, or switch on a certain part of the machine.

A water pump

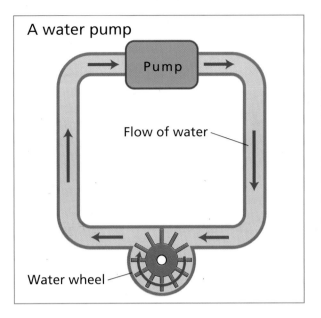

An electrical circuit

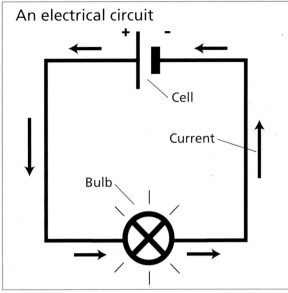

You can use a mental picture of a pump pushing water around a pipe to help you imagine how electricity flows through a circuit. Since no water escapes from the pipe, the same amount of water returns to the pump as leaves it. In the same way, the size of an electric current returning to the cell is the same as the size of the current anywhere else in the circuit.

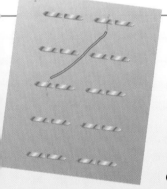

3. Turn the card over. Cut a length of wire and connect the fastener next to the top sum to the fastener next to its correct answer. Repeat for the other problems and answers.

4. Cut three more lengths of wire. Connect the ends of two of them to the terminals of the battery and connect the other end of one of them to the bulb holder. Connect the other length of wire to the opposite side of the bulb holder.

5. Get a friend to touch the fastener next to the top problem with one of the bare wires and use the other bare wire to touch the fastener next to the answer that he or she thinks is correct. Does the bulb light? How many problems does your friend answer correctly?

TURN IT ON

A switch acts like a bridge in a circuit. When a switch is 'on', or 'closed', the circuit is completed and electrons can cross the bridge. When the circuit is switched off, the bridge is 'opened' and the electric current cannot flow.

Computers contain a vast number of switches, from the keys on the keyboard to those within the computer itself, operating devices such as the printer.

If you look around your home you will find push-button switches on your television or radio, pull switches in bathrooms and pressure-sensitive switches under each key on a computer keyboard. Some switches are sensitive to movement, and are called tilt switches and tremble switches. Other switches, called two-way switches, can be used to turn lights on and off at both the top and bottom of the stairs. The brightness of a light can be changed using a dimmer switch, which alters the amount of current that goes through the lighting circuit.

Switches called relays turn on the current in one circuit as the current in another is turned off. Relay switches are used in the starter motors of cars and can also be used to close the curtains of a room when it gets dark!

If a magnet is used to switch the current from one circuit to the other, it is called a reed switch.

Did you know?

The detectors contained in outdoor security lights and burglar alarms inside houses are sensitive to infrared light (which we cannot see) from sources such as a moving person. If an intruder crosses a room, the detector senses the change in infrared radiation and sounds the alarm.

BURGLAR ALARM

1. At the corners of both sheets of card, glue a small piece of sponge foam. In the middle of both sheets, glue a small piece of aluminium foil about 10 cm x 8 cm.

2. Force a paper fastener through each piece of foil and open up the arms on the other side of each sheet of card.

3. Wind the bared ends of two long pieces of insulated wire around the open arms of both paper fasteners. Attach the other ends of the wires to the battery and the buzzer or bulb in its holder. Then connect the battery to the bulb or buzzer with another length of wire to make a circuit.

4. Lay one sheet of card on top of the other and place both sheets under a mat or carpet inside a doorway. Check that the alarm works by stepping on to the carpet above the card 'switch'. Also check that the alarm stops when you step off the carpet.

5. Your alarm is now set to go off whenever someone comes into the room. Can you think of anywhere else in the room where a similar alarm could be fitted? Try designing other switches that could be used as part of an alarm circuit.

SERIES AND PARALLEL

There are two basic sorts of electric circuit – series and parallel. All the components in a series circuit are joined to the cell by a single loop of wire. Current flows through each component in turn and back to the cell. The more bulbs there are, the dimmer their light will be, because they all have to share the voltage from the cell. In a circuit with two bulbs to one cell, each bulb would be 'half-of-one-cell bright'. If one of the bulbs fails, the entire circuit is broken and all of the bulbs will go out.

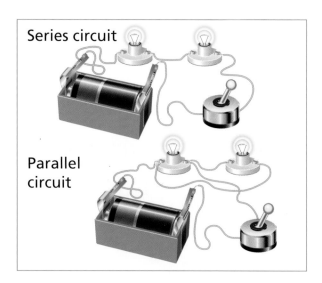

Series circuit

Parallel circuit

CONNECTIONS

This project involves testing a friend to see if he or she can work out how you have connected some bulbs and switches. For this reason, do not let your friend see you carry out steps **1** to **4**.

1. Construct a series circuit that includes two bulbs and two switches, and using three of the cells. Sketch how the circuit should look first.

2. Place the components of your series circuit on one of the sheets of card. Make holes in the card and loop the wires underneath the sheet to connect the components.

3. Tape the wires to the sheet to keep them in place. Leave two trailing wires to connect to the battery.

4. Construct a parallel circuit with the other bulbs, switches and cells. Sketch your circuit design first because there are two different ways to connect these components in parallel. The position of the switches in the circuit will decide whether no bulbs, one bulb or both bulbs light.

MATERIALS

- two sheets of stiff card (20 cm x 15 cm)
- a reel of insulated wire
- crocodile clips
- sticky tape
- scissors
- six 1.5-volt cells and holders
- four bulbs and holders
- four switches
- a screwdriver

In a parallel circuit, each bulb is in a separate branch, so each has its own connection to the cell. This means that each bulb gets the full voltage of the source and, if there is one cell, each bulb will get one cell's worth of voltage and will be 'one-cell' bright. Current leaving the cell is split, with part going down each branch. If there are two bulbs, each bulb will receive half the current, three bulbs would receive a third, and so on. The individual currents then come together again and return to the opposite terminal of the cell. If one of the bulbs fails, it breaks only its branch of the circuit, and the others will carry on shining as brightly as before.

The bulbs in this Christmas tree are in a parallel circuit, so that if one blows, the others will carry on shining.

In a series circuit, opposite (top), the bulbs share the voltage 'push' of the cell. In a parallel circuit, opposite (bottom), the full voltage reaches each bulb. Removing a bulb will help to identify the type of circuit used.

5. Repeat step **2**, leaving two bare wires to connect to the battery.

6. Ask your friend to work out how the bulbs and switches are connected in each circuit by turning the switches on and off, and by observing the brightness of the bulbs.

Decide if you will allow your friend to remove one of the bulbs during the testing. He or she should sketch how the components might be connected. Compare your friend's drawings with your own. How similar are they?

CIRCUIT DIAGRAMS

As more components are included in a circuit, it becomes difficult to describe by using sketches. Circuit diagrams are a 'shorthand' way of drawing circuits that show the path the electric current takes along the wires.

This chart shows some of the common components used to build electric circuits and the symbols that represent them. Some will be used later in the book.

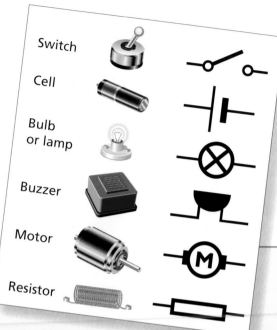

Switch

Cell

Bulb or lamp

Buzzer

Motor

Resistor

CIRCUIT SNAP

1. Cut up one large sheet of card into 20 smaller cards. On each one draw a picture of an electrical component from the list above. Then write its name underneath it. You will have to repeat the components several times. These are your 'Name' cards.

Bulb

Name card

2. Cut up the other large sheet of card in the same way. On each one draw the symbol for one of the components you have available. These are your 'Symbol' cards.

3. Cut up the small sheet of card into four large cards. Draw four different circuit diagrams that make use of the electrical components you have. Make two of the circuits series and two parallel. These are your 'Build-it' cards.

4. One player keeps the Name cards, the other the Symbol cards. Place the Build-it cards face down in the middle of the table, with the electrical components within easy reach of both players.

MATERIALS
- two sheets of card (297 cm x 420 cm) in different colours
- one sheet of card (210 cm x 297 cm) in another colour
- scissors
- two or three 1.5-volt cells and holders
- two switches
- three bulbs and holders
- one buzzer
- lengths of insulated wire

There are certain rules to follow when drawing circuit diagrams. First, cells should be shown connected the right way round, that is positive terminal to negative.

Second, connecting wires should be shown as single straight lines at right angles to each other. It doesn't matter what kind of bulb holder, switch or cell you use – the symbols are always the same. And it doesn't matter how you connect the components, whether by twisting wires together or by using crocodile clips. These are not shown on the diagram.

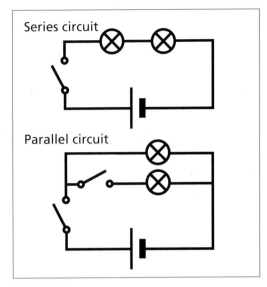

Series circuit

Parallel circuit

5. The players each turn over the top card from their pile. If the cards match, the first player to shout 'Snap' keeps the two cards. If the cards do not match, put them face down to one side in separate Name and Symbol piles.

6. When all the cards have been turned over, the player with fewest tricks takes a Build-it card and constructs the circuit from the components.

7. The players shuffle the remaining cards in their separate piles and start the game again. When all the Build-it cards are used up and all the others turned over, the winner is the player with the most tricks.

Symbol card

Build-it card

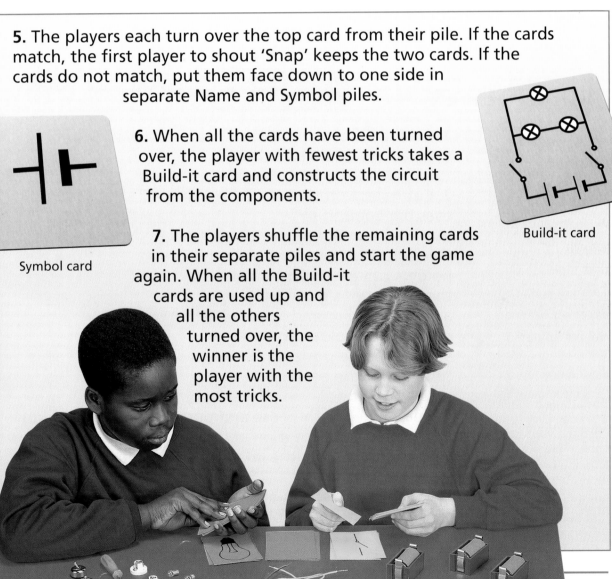

CONDUCTIVITY

An electric current flows when electrons can move freely along a wire. The atoms in some metals have a number of electrons that are not held very strongly by the nuclei of the atoms. Such electrons tend to drift away and

Electricity comes to our homes through thick metal cables attached to electricity pylons. To stop currents crossing from the cables to the pylons, we use insulators made from a ceramic material, rather like that used to make coffee mugs.

ROBOT TESTER

MATERIALS

- a shoe box
- three 1.5-volt cells and holders
- two bulbs and holders
- a switch
- sticky tape
- scissors or craft knife
- two paper fasteners
- a reel of insulated wire
- materials to test to see how well they conduct electricity, such as a silver spoon, a badge, wool, cotton, a nail, a brass screw, pens, kitchen foil
- coloured pens or pencils

1. On the lid of the shoe box draw a face, with two eyes, a nose and a mouth.

2. Cut holes in the eyes big enough to push the two bulbs through. The bulb holders can go under the lid, out of sight. Cut a length of wire and connect the holders in series with the positive terminal of the battery.

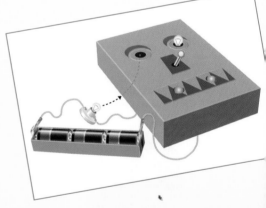

3. Cut a hole for the nose and push the switch through so that you can turn it on and off easily. Fix the switch to the underside of the lid with sticky tape.

4. Cut another length of wire and connect the switch in series with the bulb holders.

move about at random in the metal. These metals are conductors. In most materials, however, electrons are held near the nucleus; these materials are insulators. Although all metals are conductors, some conductors are better than others. Copper, for example, is a very good conductor. Because of this it is often used in electrical wiring.

Other substances also allow electric current to pass through them. Graphite (pencil 'lead') conducts electricity and is used in some electric motors. Some liquids can also conduct electricity, which is why it is dangerous to let water come into contact with a machine powered by electricity, especially if you are holding it – you conduct electricity, too! Gases are poor conductors, but if the current is big enough, an electric spark will jump a gap between two good conductors.

Wood, plastic, glass and paper do not let electric currents pass through them very easily, because their atoms have very few 'loose' electrons. Such materials are called electrical insulators, which is why copper wires have a plastic coating to stop electric currents jumping from one wire to another whenever they touch.

5. Push the two paper fasteners down through the mouth shape on the lid, so that they look like two gold teeth. Bend out the arms of the fasteners to hold them in place. Now cut a length of wire to connect one fastener in series with the other end of the switch, and a final length of wire to join the arms of the second fastener back to the negative terminal of the battery.

6. Use sticky tape to attach the wires to the underside of the lid, and place the lid on to the box. Your robot is ready to be fed!

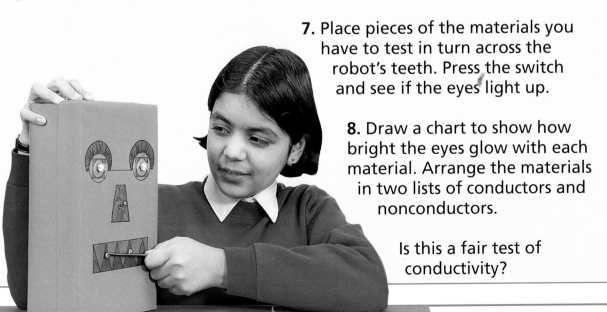

7. Place pieces of the materials you have to test in turn across the robot's teeth. Press the switch and see if the eyes light up.

8. Draw a chart to show how bright the eyes glow with each material. Arrange the materials in two lists of conductors and nonconductors.

Is this a fair test of conductivity?

RESISTANCE

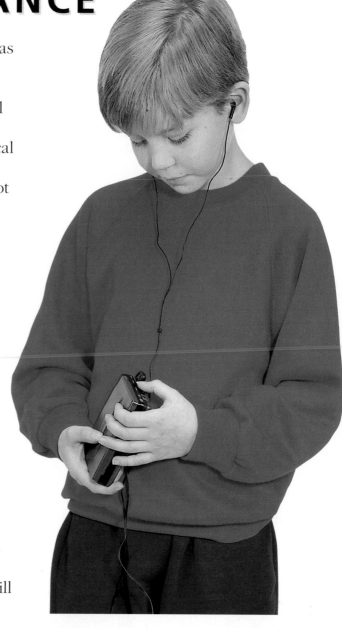

Good conductors of electricity, such as metals and graphite, allow electric currents to pass through them easily. This means they have a low electrical resistance. Most non-metals, such as rubber or plastic, have a high electrical resistance. If they are connected to a cell, the electrons from the cell cannot move through the material because they bump into its atoms and are slowed down. This is what happens inside insulators.

On page 14 you read that the water pipe model can help to explain how current flows through a circuit. You can think of the components, such as bulbs and buzzers, as being like small sponges inside the pipe, soaking up the current and resisting – but not stopping – the flow. So, for any size of cell or battery, the size of the current that flows in the circuit is decided by the resistance of the components. Components that allow large currents to flow have a low resistance, while components with a high resistance will only allow small currents to pass.

The wires in a circuit also affect resistance. Long wires should be avoided in circuits because the longer the wire, the more metal atoms there are for the electrons to collide with, and so the greater the resistance. Also, very thin wires should be avoided in circuits, because there is less room for the electrons to squeeze through, and

The volume control on a personal stereo is a variable resistor. This is a device that changes the length of wire through which the current passes – a shorter wire means less resistance and louder sound.

so the resistance increases. Thick wires have a larger cross-sectional area and so let through more electrons, which means more current.

DIMMER SWITCH

1. Use the insulated wires to make a circuit with the battery, the bulb and the switch. Twist the bare ends of the wires around the nails.

2. Take each length of nichrome wire and, in turn, place them across the gap between the two nails. Switch on the current. What happens to the brightness of the bulb?

3. Now coil the longest nichrome wire around the pencil about 20 times.

4. Attach one end of the coil of nichrome wire to one of the two nails.

5. Touch the coil at different points along its length against the other nail and switch on. What do you notice?

You have made a variable resistor. It takes the place of lots of different lengths of wire with different amounts of electrical resistance. Variable resistors are found in dimmer switches for room lights and in volume controls on radios and televisions.

PRODUCING HEAT

You will probably have noticed that, in the project on page 25, the nichrome wire warms up if you leave the current flowing for more than a few seconds. This is the heating effect of an electric current and is one of the most important uses of electricity.

Electric cookers and heaters change electrical energy into heat energy by forcing electric currents through wires or plates that are made from conducting materials with a high resistance. The loose electrons that carry the electric current bump into atoms of these materials, making them vibrate and bump into other atoms, generating heat energy. To help the conductor give out its heat over a longer time, it is usually covered with a coating of a material that can store heat.

A conductor gets hotter as you pass more current through it. One way of increasing the current is to increase the voltage of the electricity supply. But eventually, the atoms of the conductor are vibrating as quickly as they can, and an increase in the voltage will not produce any extra heat.

To produce enough heat to melt the iron inside this electric furnace, an electricity supply is required equal to that needed to boil 30,000 kettles.

The connection between voltage and current is called the power of the device. This is measured in watts (or thousands of watts, called kilowatts) and is found by multiplying the voltage of the device by the current that can pass through it.

HOT-WIRE CUTTER

1. Nail the two 30 cm lengths of wood onto the sheet so that they are standing approximately 10 cm apart.

2. Knock a nail into the top of each of these vertical wooden supports and wind the ends of the nichrome wire around each one, so that it is stretched between them.

3. Attach crocodile clips to one end of two lengths of insulated wire. Place one clip on one end of the nichrome wire and connect the other end to one terminal of the battery. Use the second length of insulated wire to connect the other end of the nichrome wire to a switch. Cut a third piece of insulated wire to connect the other terminal of the battery to the switch.

MATERIALS

- a 15 cm length of nichrome wire
- a 6-volt battery
- a switch
- a reel of insulated wire
- two crocodile clips
- two 30 cm long lengths of 2 cm square section wood or dowel rod
- a 25-30 cm square sheet of wood
- nails and a hammer
- a polystyrene tile
- a pencil
- card and coloured pens

WARNING

- Always carry out this project with an adult present as the wire may get very hot.

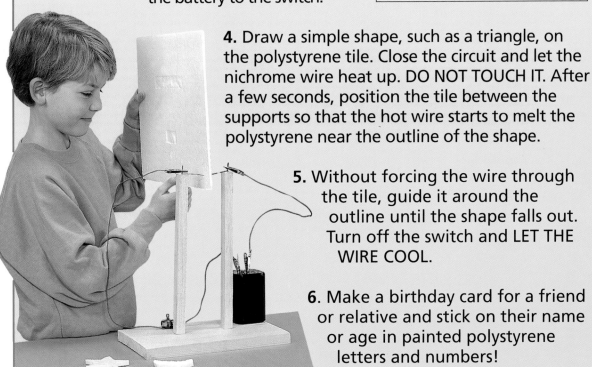

4. Draw a simple shape, such as a triangle, on the polystyrene tile. Close the circuit and let the nichrome wire heat up. DO NOT TOUCH IT. After a few seconds, position the tile between the supports so that the hot wire starts to melt the polystyrene near the outline of the shape.

5. Without forcing the wire through the tile, guide it around the outline until the shape falls out. Turn off the switch and LET THE WIRE COOL.

6. Make a birthday card for a friend or relative and stick on their name or age in painted polystyrene letters and numbers!

ELECTRIC LIGHT

When an electric current passes through a wire, the atoms not only produce heat when they resist the movement of electrons, they may also change some of the electrical energy into light. Light bulbs contain very thin wires, called filaments, which force the electrons to travel through an extremely small area. The resistance is further increased by making the wire very long and coiling it up to fit into a small space. The wire resists the current so much that the filament becomes hot enough to glow white.

If the filament were made of a metal such as copper it would melt, so a metal called tungsten is used, which can glow white-hot without melting. Also, if the bulb contained air, the filament would react with the gases in the air and burn away instantly, ruining the bulb. Instead, the filament is surrounded by inert gases such as nitrogen or argon, which do not react with it. By varying the gas mixture inside the bulb, the colour of the light from the bulb can be changed. For example, lamps containing the element sodium give a yellow light that improves visibility in foggy conditions.

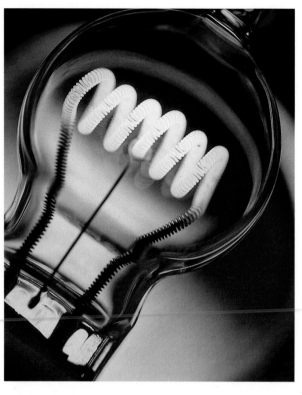

The resistance of the wire filament inside a light bulb must be low enough for it to glow when current passes through it, but not so low that it burns right through.

Like other electrical devices, household light bulbs have the power they use written on the glass, such as 40 W (watts), which is quite dim, up to 150 W, which is extremely bright. Light bulbs that are not used with mains voltage, such as the bulbs used in the projects in this book, have the current they can pass stamped on the side instead of the power they consume.

LIGHTING SURVEY

1. Using the squared paper as a guide, make a map to show where the light bulbs are in your home. Draw the rooms roughly to scale.

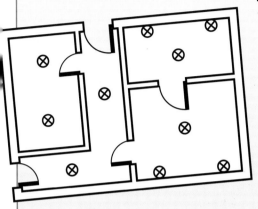

2. Look at each of the bulbs in all the rooms and write down as much information as possible about the

bulbs, such as how the bulb fits into the socket – is it bayonet or screw-fitting? What is the power rating of each bulb? Does the bulb have a reflective coating? What shape is the bulb – mushroom or round? Or is it a fluorescent tube?

3. Make up a key for your room map, using your coloured pencils, so that whenever a bulb 'goes', anyone can check your chart to see what sort of bulb they need to replace it. Pin up your chart near to where the spare bulbs are kept.

Did you know?

Most electric light bulbs waste 95 per cent of the electrical energy that passes through them as heat. Only 5 per cent is actually changed into light. Newer energy-saving fluorescent lights use about a quarter of the electricity used by ordinary light bulbs, and last up to 13 times longer.

29

ELECTROLYSIS

An electric current is not always made up of moving electrons. Other electrically charged particles, called ions, can also carry a current. Water contains the elements hydrogen (H) and oxygen (O), which can form two sorts of ion – positively charged hydrogen ions, written as H+, and negatively charged hydroxide ions, written as OH–. When certain solid substances are dissolved in water they also take the form of ions. In the case of a solution of table salt, which has the chemical name sodium chloride, there are positively charged sodium ions and negatively charged chloride ions in the water.

If two carbon rods are connected to the terminals of a battery, they become what are called electrodes. The electrode connected to the positive terminal is known as the anode, while the negative electrode is the cathode. When the electrodes are dipped into a salt solution, the positively charged sodium and

Did you know?

There are not enough ions in pure water for an electric current to flow, but tap water contains a number of dissolved chemicals that can conduct electricity. This is why it can be very dangerous to handle electrical equipment if you have wet hands. Even sweaty hands can conduct enough current to give you a shock!

LIQUID CONDUCTORS

1. Set up the circuit shown below. Test that the circuit works in water only, by touching the ends of the wires together and lighting up the bulb.

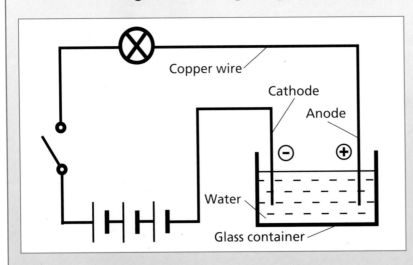

Copper wire

Cathode

Anode

Water

Glass container

MATERIALS

- three 1.5-volt cells and holders
- four lengths of insulated copper wire with bared ends
- a switch
- a bulb and holder
- crocodile clips
- washing soda
- a glass jar, a beaker or a small aquarium
- water

hydrogen ions move towards the cathode. Although the sodium ions stay in the solution, the hydrogen ions join together in pairs and become molecules of hydrogen gas, appearing as bubbles rising to the surface near the cathode.

At the anode, the hydroxide ions join up to make bubbles of oxygen gas (and water), while pairs of chloride ions get together to make chlorine – a poisonous gas! The stronger the salt solution, the more chlorine gas is formed. Scientists call this process of using electricity to split substances to make new ones electrolysis. It is used in the chemical industry to make pure substances, especially metals such as sodium and potassium.

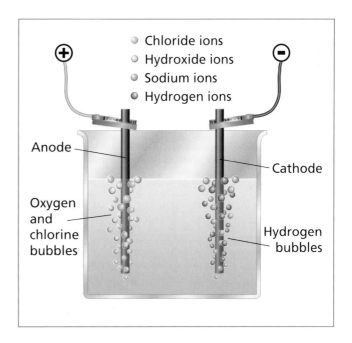

- Chloride ions
- Hydroxide ions
- Sodium ions
- Hydrogen ions

Anode

Cathode

Oxygen and chlorine bubbles

Hydrogen bubbles

During electrolysis, charged particles called ions move towards the electrodes. The positive ions collect electrons when they reach the negative electrode (or cathode), while the negative ions give up electrons when they arrive at the positive electrode (or anode).

2. Pour some washing soda into the water and stir it to dissolve it. Turn on the switch again and look for bubbles of gas rising next to the wires.

3. How brightly does the bulb shine compared with the circuit test in Step **1**? What happens to the brightness of the bulb if you stir more washing soda into the solution?

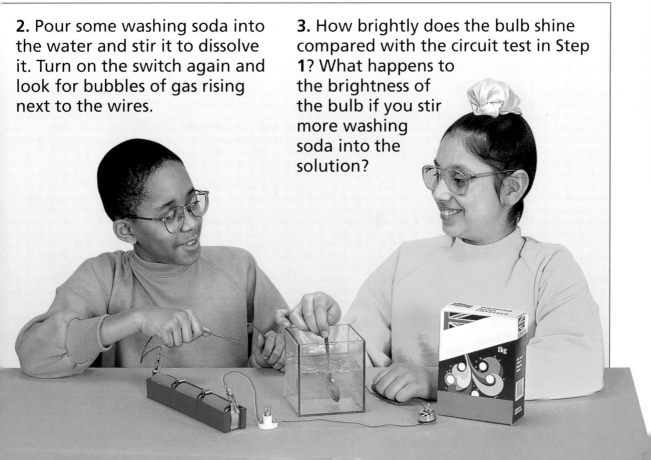

ELECTROPLATING

One important use of the electrolysis process is known as electroplating. Electroplating consists of covering one metal, often a cheap one like iron or steel, with a thin coat of another that is usually more expensive. Not only does this give an attractive appearance to the metal object, it also helps to protect the item from rusting.

The object to be electroplated is connected to a supply of electricity so that it acts as the cathode (negative electrode). The anode (positive electrode) consists of the metal that will become the coating for the object. The solution, or electrolyte, in the vessel where the reaction takes place contains the same metal as the coating – this reduces the energy needed to start the plating process. The electrolyte contains a compound of tin, in the case of tinplating a steel can, or a compound containing silver, in the case of silverplating cutlery and trophies. In the electronics industry, printed circuit boards are dipped into a solution of copper sulphate. Copper ions are attracted to the boards, where they form the copper 'tracks' that will carry electric current between the components on the board.

Anodizing is a similar process to electroplating. This uses electricity to produce oxygen bubbles on the surface of an aluminium object. The oxygen and aluminium react together to form a coat of aluminium oxide.

Fine items of silver-plated steel are popular as a cheaper alternative to solid silver.

Did you know?

The hulls of most ships are made of steel, but certain other parts that are under water are made from brass, which contains copper. In sea water, which is salty, an imbalance of electrons between the steel and the copper creates a small electric current that flows through the water between them, as though they were electrodes. This would eventually damage the brass parts. To prevent this happening, a plate of zinc is attached to the hull, which attracts the current in preference to the copper. When the zinc plate has nearly dissolved, it is replaced.

COPPER PLATING

1. Half fill the glass jar with white vinegar and add table salt to it until no more will dissolve.

2. Use a crocodile clip to connect the object to be plated to the negative terminal of the battery.

3. Use a crocodile clip to connect the positive terminal of the battery to the piece of copper.

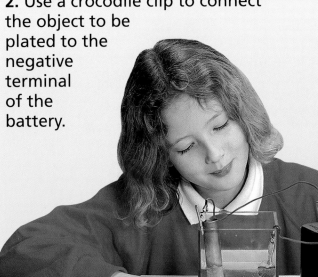

4. Place the object and the piece of copper in the jar of solution, making sure that the crocodile clips are not dipping into it.

5. What do you notice happening to the object? Shake off any bubbles you see on the object.

6. How long does it take for the object to be covered with copper? What happens to the piece of copper during that time?

ELECTROMAGNETISM

When a current flows through a wire, it creates a magnetic field around the wire. The field is strongest close to the wire, and if the wire is coiled, the magnetic field behaves like the field around a magnet, with a north pole at one end and a south pole at the other.

If an object that can be made into a magnet is placed inside a coil of wire while a current is flowing, it becomes an electromagnet. An electromagnet

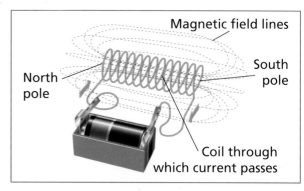

If you pass electricity along a coil of wire, a magnetic field is created at right angles to the direction of the current.

CURRENT BALANCE

1. Make the stand for the current balance by cutting a square section of wood and nailing it to the base, as shown in the picture below.

2. Cut a 15 cm strip of card and shape one end to make a pointer. Attach this to the wooden upright by pinning it about 3-4 cm from the blunt end. The card pointer should be able to turn easily around the pin.

3. Use sticky tape to suspend the nail from a cotton thread about 3-4 cm from the pointed end of the pointer.

MATERIALS

- a reel of insulated wire
- a nail
- three 1.5-volt cells and holders
- a switch
- modelling clay
- cotton thread
- a sheet of stiff card 20 cm x 20 cm
- a ruler and scissors
- sticky tape and wood glue
- two pins and a hammer
- crocodile clips
- a 20 cm length of square section wood for stand
- a sheet of wood for the base

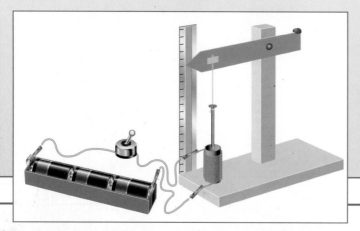

4. Add modelling clay to the blunt end of the strip of card so that the pointer balances.

will attract other magnetic objects while the current continues to flow. A steel nail still behaves like a magnet even after the current has been switched off, whereas an iron nail loses magnetism when the current stops flowing. This property of iron is a useful feature in scrapyards, allowing heavy metal objects to be picked up and moved by huge electromagnets, which release them again when the current is switched off.

A problem with large electromagnets is that they produce a lot of heat because of the high resistance to the current flowing through the wire coils. Scientists have discovered a group of substances that, at extremely low temperatures, do not have any resistance to the flow of electric currents. Electromagnets made from these materials, called superconductors, do not waste electrical energy as heat and so they can be made smaller, but just as powerful. Trains have been designed using these superconducting electromagnets, which will travel on a magnetic field 'cushion' at speeds of up to 350 kilometres per hour.

5. Cut a 4 cm square of card and roll it up to make a tube slightly wider than the thickness of the nail. Wind insulated wire tightly around the tube to make a coil, leaving two ends bare.

6. Use modelling clay to fix the card tube to the stand below the nail, making sure that the nail hangs just inside the tube without touching the sides. You may need to adjust the length of the thread at this stage.

7. Use crocodile clips to attach connecting wires to the coil and make a circuit with the switch and the battery.

8. Switch on the current and see what happens to the pointer. You have made an electromagnetic current measurer.

9. Use the ruler to measure how much the pointer moves. How does adding or taking away a cell affect the movement of the pointer?

What happens if you add a bulb to the circuit?

ELECTRIC MOTORS

You have seen that when an electric current passes along a wire, a magnetic field is created around it. If this takes place near to another magnetic field, produced by a magnet, the magnetic fields affect each other to produce either a pulling or a pushing force on the wire, depending on the direction of the current. This force is used in electric motors, such as you find in many household appliances.

In an electric motor, the magnetic field is created between two facing sides – the north and south poles – of a magnet. The wire is wound into a flat coil, which is fixed to a rod so that it can turn. When the coil is fixed between the poles of the magnet and a current is passed through the coil, the force on the coil makes it turn until the north pole of the magnet lines up with

The batteries that power the motor for this electric car are charged by solar cells on the roof of the owner's house.

the south pole of the magnetic field around the coil.

At that point, halfway through a complete turn, an attachment (the commutator) on the rod that carries the coil reverses the direction that the current flows though the wire, and the north and south poles of the magnetic field instantly swap places. Now that the north pole of the field around the coil is facing the north pole of the magnet – and the same goes for the south poles – like poles repel and the coil carries on turning. This reversal of the direction the current takes through the coil happens twice in each turn, so that the coil keeps spinning between the poles of the magnet. The turning movement of the rod that supports the coil can be used to turn other things, including the gears and belts that drive the machines we use.

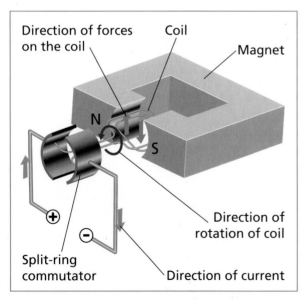

Direction of forces on the coil
Coil
Magnet
N
S
Direction of rotation of coil
Split-ring commutator
Direction of current

This diagram shows the main parts of an electric motor.

SIMPLE MOTOR

1. Ask an adult to push the knitting needle through the corks.

2. Wind copper wire about 20 times around the large corks, using two drawing pins in each end to hold the coil together. Bare the ends and tape them to either side of the smaller cork.

3. Hammer the nails at angles into the baseboard so that they cross. Balance the knitting needle between them, making sure that it can turn freely.

MATERIALS

- two large corks and one small cork
- a thin knitting needle
- two bar magnets with polarized faces
- insulated copper wire
- two wooden blocks to support magnets
- four nails
- a switch
- a 6-volt battery
- three insulated connecting wires
- a wooden base board
- a hammer
- sticky tape

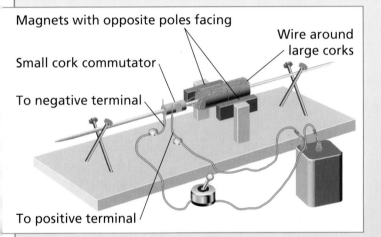

Magnets with opposite poles facing

Wire around large corks

Small cork commutator

To negative terminal

To positive terminal

4. Tape the two magnets to the tops of the wooden blocks placed either side of the large cork, so that they are level with the coil. Make sure that the magnets have opposite poles facing each other.

5. Construct the circuit shown in the diagram. Make sure that the bared ends of the connecting wires leading from the battery and the switch to the small cork press against the two taped ends of the wire coil, by holding them down with drawing pins.

6. Switch on the current and watch your motor turn. (You may need to give it a spin with your fingers to start it off.)

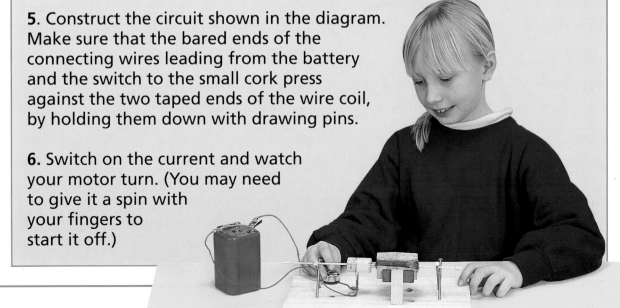

GENERATORS

You have read that passing an electric current through a wire can produce a magnetic field around the wire. If, instead, a wire is moved through the field of a magnet, a current can be produced inside the wire. The size of that current depends on how quickly the wire moves. All devices that generate electricity make use of this effect. Many bicycles, for example, use a generator called a dynamo to change the movement energy of a wheel into electrical energy for the bicycle lamp.

In a dynamo, a coil mounted between the poles of a magnet is made to spin. As the coil spins, a current is generated

within the coil. Because the current is always moving in the same direction through the coil, it is called direct current (dc), just as the current that is

In this power station, steam is forced into a giant turbine, which turns an electromagnet inside the blue cylinder. This produces enough power for a small town.

ELECTRICITY PRODUCER

1. Place the compass in the tray of the matchbox. Wind one end of the wire 15 to 20 times around the matchbox tray.

2. Roll the card around the piece of broom handle to make a cylinder and tape it in place. Wind the other end of the wire around the card and broom handle at least 50 times to make a second coil. Tape it at both ends to keep it in place.

3. Connect the two ends of the wire together, but keep the broom handle coil well clear of the compass.

MATERIALS
- a 5 m reel of insulated wire
- a strong bar magnet
- a magnetic compass
- a small box
- a 30 cm section of broom handle
- a small piece of card
- sticky tape

produced by a cell is direct. But it is not a steady current. Unlike the current from a cell, the current from a dc dynamo changes in size as the coil turns. By altering the electrical connections to the coil, the current can be made to change direction twice in every complete turn of the coil. This is called alternating current (ac) and the current that flows from our mains supply is like this.

The same principle is used in power station generators, except that it is the magnet that turns inside the coil, not the other way round. Steam at very high pressure is made to turn turbines, which are connected to powerful electromagnets. As the electromagnets spin, they generate electricity in the fixed coils around them. The more turns made on the coil, and the faster the magnet spins, the larger the voltage generated.

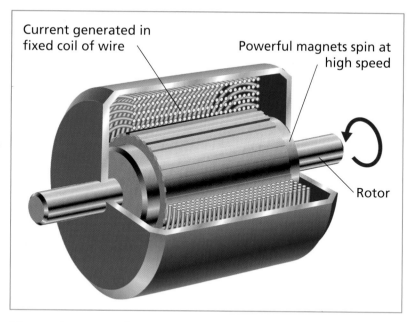

Current generated in fixed coil of wire

Powerful magnets spin at high speed

Rotor

The main parts of a generator can be seen in this diagram. This kind of generator is used in power stations.

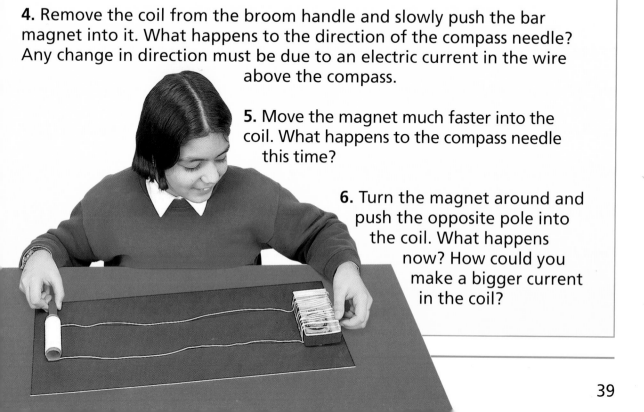

4. Remove the coil from the broom handle and slowly push the bar magnet into it. What happens to the direction of the compass needle? Any change in direction must be due to an electric current in the wire above the compass.

5. Move the magnet much faster into the coil. What happens to the compass needle this time?

6. Turn the magnet around and push the opposite pole into the coil. What happens now? How could you make a bigger current in the coil?

ELECTRICITY SUPPLY

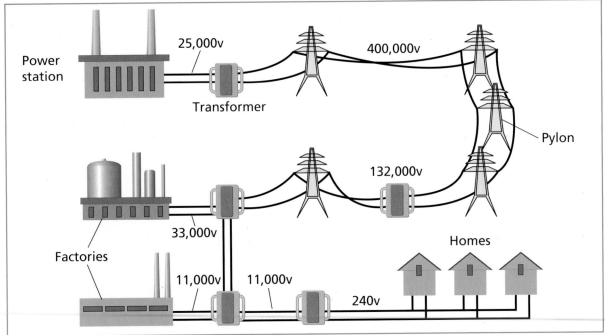

Power station · 25,000v · Transformer · 400,000v · Pylon · Factories · 132,000v · 33,000v · Homes · 11,000v · 11,000v · 240v

Power stations send electricity through long wires, or cables, to the places where we live and work. Some of these cables are many kilometres long and very thick, while those that we use to connect our appliances to the wall sockets that supply mains electricity are lighter and much more flexible.

As a wire becomes longer, its resistance to the flow of electric current becomes greater. The big problem with sending electricity over long distances is how to overcome the loss of power caused by this resistance. Scientists discovered that you can deliver the same electrical power without much being wasted if you increase the voltage and decrease the current in the cable. This change to the voltage produced by the power station is achieved by a transformer.

Electricity is made in a power station and passes through a number of stages to reach its destination, such as a factory, a hospital or your home.

Transformers are needed not only to increase the voltage of the electricity supply when it leaves the power station but also to decrease it again by different amounts to suit the needs of different consumers, such as factories or homes.

When electricity reaches the place where it will be used, it goes through a meter. This measures and records how much is consumed, so that the electricity company knows how much money the customer must pay. Once inside, a junction box sends the electricity along a number of circuits to different parts of the building.

METER CHECK

1. Ask an adult to show you the electricity meter for your home. It may have several round dials or it may have a single display. The measurement of electricity used will be in 'kWh', or kilowatt hours.

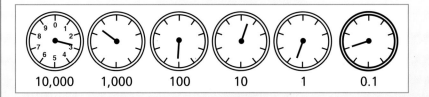

| 10,000 | 1,000 | 100 | 10 | 1 | 0.1 |

MATERIALS

- three or four electrical appliances
- a torch
- a clock or watch
- a pencil

2. Check that you can read what number the meter is showing, and write down the meter reading. Look at the meter again after five minutes. Write down the new reading. Is there a noticeable difference between the two readings? (The only figures likely to have changed are the last two on the right.)

3. Ask an adult to turn on an item of electrical equipment, such as an electric cooker or fire, an electric kettle, a vacuum cleaner or a hairdryer. Ask the adult to turn off the appliance after five minutes.

4. Look at the meter again, and write down the new reading. What has happened this time?

5. Repeat the experiment using two or three other appliances. If the results are different, why might this be?

6. By taking readings from your meter, find out how much electricity is used in your home over a day and over a week. Ask an adult to tell you how much each kilowatt hour, or unit, of electricity costs. Can you work out what your weekly electricity supply costs?

KEEPING SAFE

Electric shocks are an obvious hazard associated with the use of electricity, but they are not the only danger. Many deaths and injuries also result from electrical fires caused by connecting too many appliances to one circuit. One of the most important safety components in a mains circuit is the fuse, and there are several of them in a fusebox close to where the electricity supply enters a building. Each one contains a wire so thin that if the current gets too big, the wire will get hot enough to melt, or 'blow', and break the circuit. This will prevent appliances inside the building receiving a current higher than they can stand, which could make them overheat.

Not every appliance connected to a home wall socket draws the same current. The current that some devices require may be much less than the maximum available, and so plugs should also contain a fuse that will 'blow' when the current exceeds the safe limit of the device.

Fuses will also blow if there is a short circuit. This may happen if an electrical device is faulty or damaged.

Appliances that need a mains electricity supply use plugs that slide into the holes in a wall socket. The pins are connected to the wires inside the plug, which are, in turn, connected to the electrical parts of the appliance.

When an electric kettle, for example, is plugged in and switched on, the current flows between the live wire and the neutral wire. Sometimes there is a third wire. This is called the earth wire. It provides a connection from the metal case of the kettle to the earth, so that if the live wire accidentally touches the case, the current will flow to earth and not through a person touching the kettle. This is what is meant by an electrical appliance being 'earthed'.

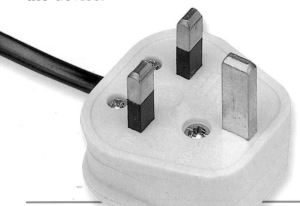

FUSES

1. Use the connecting wires to link one crocodile clip to the switch and another to a terminal of the battery. Connect the other terminal of the battery to the switch.

2. Cut equal lengths of fuse wire and select a strand of steel wool of about the same length.

3. Connect one piece of wire between the jaws of the crocodile clips and place it on the wooden sheet. Switch on the current.

4. Observe what happens but DO NOT TOUCH THE WIRE. IT COULD BE HOT. Do not leave the switch on for more than a few seconds, or you will drain the battery.

Did you know?

Some houses have devices called circuit breakers, or trip switches, fitted to the mains circuits or into individual wall sockets. If the current drawn from the socket or the supply changes suddenly, a switch inside the circuit breaker will quickly cut off the current to the appliance. This is very important when using a device such as an electric lawnmower or drill, which could damage the mains cable and risk giving an electric shock.

5. Repeat the tests for the other lengths of fuse wire and the strand of steel wool. Which ones are able to carry the current without being damaged? What is the pattern that connects the thickness of the fuse wire and the size of the current it can pass?

ELECTRONICS

Electronics is about controlling the flow of electrons to make things happen. Once an electronic device is connected to an electricity supply, the current is controlled by electronic switches. Most modern washing machines, for example, are electronically controlled, making them 'automatic'.

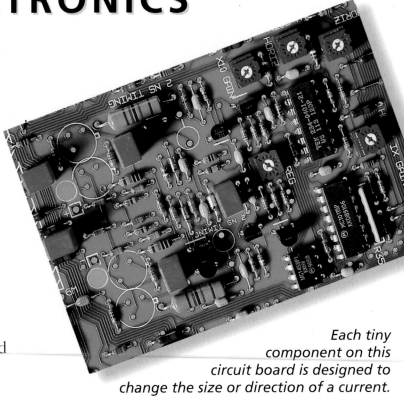

Each tiny component on this circuit board is designed to change the size or direction of a current.

The parts of an electronic device that 'turn on' electronic switches are called sensors. A sensor detects changes in its surroundings, such as the amount of light in front of an automatic camera. When light levels are low it sends a signal to the flash unit, telling it to operate the flash when a picture is taken.

The electronic switches that receive 'on' or 'off' signals from the sensors are called logic gates, because they control how current moves around a circuit according to a set of rules, or logic. Logic gates are simple circuits made up of electronic components called transistors. The action of the gate – that is, whether it lets a current pass or not – depends on how the transistors are connected.

There are three basic sorts of gate, called the NOT, the OR and the AND gates. All types of logic gate respond to a signal from a sensor (the input) and produce a signal of their own (the output).

The type of electronic switch known as a NOT gate is the simplest of all. It produces an output signal when it does NOT receive an input signal. The table shows how the action of the NOT gate can be written. This type of table is called a truth table.

NOT gate

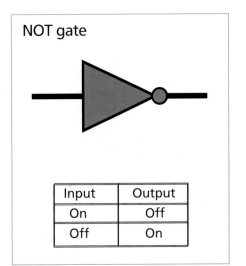

Input	Output
On	Off
Off	On

AND gate

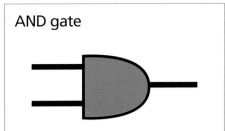

Input A	Input B	Output
Off	Off	Off
Off	On	Off
On	Off	Off
On	On	On

AND and OR logic gates can receive two or more input signals. A two-input AND gate will produce an output if it gets a signal from Input A AND Input B. A two-input OR gate only needs input from Input A OR Input B.

OR gate

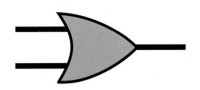

Input A	Input B	Output
Off	Off	Off
On	Off	On
Off	On	On
On	On	On

USING SENSORS

MATERIALS

- two 1.5-volt cells and holders
- two connecting wires
- an LDR (ORP12)
- an LED
- a thermistor (TH3)

A light-emitting diode (LED) is a coloured plastic-coated electronic component that gives off light when a current passes through it. Current can only pass in one direction through a diode. A light-dependent resistor (LDR) is a sensor that changes its resistance as the brightness of the surroundings changes. A thermistor is a sensor whose resistance changes with a rise or fall in temperature.

1. Connect the short leg of the LED to the negative terminal of the battery and the long leg to the LDR. Connect the LDR to the positive terminal of the battery.

2. What do you notice when you cover the LDR with your hand? Name an electrical device that could be controlled by an LDR.

3. Replace the LDR with the thermistor and hold it in your hand to make it warm.

4. What do you notice? Name an electrical device that could be controlled by a thermistor.

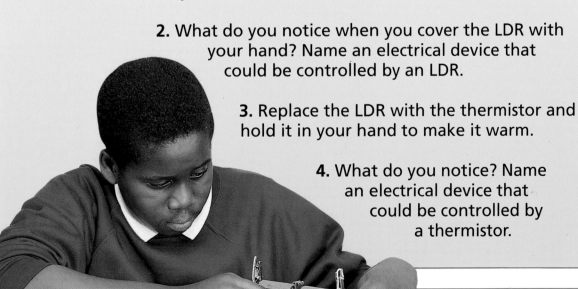

GLOSSARY

Alternating current An electric current that changes its direction many times every second.

Battery A group of cells. The voltage of a battery depends on the number of cells it contains.

Cell A source of electrical energy containing chemicals that react together to produce a voltage between two terminals.

Circuit A group of components, including a source of electrical energy, linked by material that can conduct an electric current between them.

Component An item in a circuit, such as a bulb or switch.

Conductor A material that allows electric current to pass through it. Metals are good conductors.

Current The movement of electrons, or flow of electric charge, through a conductor.

Direct current An electric current that flows in one direction only.

Earth wire A safety device that connects an electrical appliance to the earth. If a fault occurs, the current will flow to earth and melt a fuse, so breaking the circuit.

Electrodes A pair of conducting rods or plates connected to the terminals of a battery. The electrode connected to the positive terminal is called the anode, while the electrode connected to the negative terminal is called the cathode. Electrons flow from the cathode to the anode as an electric current.

Electromagnet A magnet made when magnetic material is placed inside a coil of wire through which an electric current is passing.

Electrons The small particles inside an atom that move around the larger nucleus at the centre.

Fuse A safety device consisting of a thin piece of metal wire that becomes hot and melts if the electric current becomes too strong, so breaking the circuit.

Generator A device that uses the movement of a magnet relative to a coil of conducting material to generate an electric current.

Insulator Material such as the plastic coating on a conducting wire, which resists the flow of an electric current.

Live wire The path that electric energy takes when it flows from a generator to an electrical appliance by means of an alternating current.

Logic gate An electronic switch used to control a circuit.

Neutral wire The wire that completes the circuit in which electrical energy flows from a generator to an electrical appliance by means of alternating current.

Parallel circuit An electrical circuit with several routes to and from the source.

Power Rate of transfer of energy, measured in watts.

Resistance Ease with which electrons flow through a material when it is part of a circuit.

Series circuit An electrical circuit connected in a single loop, with no branches.

Short circuit A path for electric current that has very low resistance compared with the rest of the circuit. Most of the current will pass through a short circuit.

Static electricity Collection of positive or negative charges on the surface of some materials.

Transformer Device consisting of two coils wound around an iron core. It uses an alternating voltage in one coil to produce a higher or lower voltage in the other.

Voltage The electrical energy of a battery or other source of electricity, which forces electrons through a circuit. Voltage is measured in volts and written as 'V'.

FURTHER INFORMATION

BOOKS

Eyewitness Science: Electricity Steve Parker
(Dorling Kindersley, 1992)

How Things Work Chris Oxlade
(Zigzag, 1995)

The Oxford Children's Book of Science
(Oxford University Press, 1994)

Exploring Electricity Ed Catherall
(Wayland, 1991)

CD–ROMS

The Way Things Work David Macaulay
(Dorling Kindersley)

ANSWERS TO QUESTIONS

Answers to questions posed in the projects.

Page 6 Rubbing the plastic bottle and pen gives them both a negative charge. Since negative charges repel each other, the bottle will turn away from the pen. Rubbing the glass bottle gives it a positive charge. Since negative and positive charges attract each other, the bottle will turn towards the pen.

Page 7 Rubbing the balloon increases the number of negative charges (electrons) on its surface. These repel the negative charges on the paper and attract the positive charges (protons). This force of attraction makes the stream of water bend towards the balloon.

Page 9 Rubbing the balloon increases the number of negative charges (electrons) on its surface. These repel the negative charges on the paper and attract the positive charges (protons). This force of attraction makes the snakes leap up to touch the balloon.

Page 11 Rubbing the comb or brush increases the number of negative charges (electrons) on its surface. When placed on the nail, the negative charges induce positive charges on the foil strips. They repel each other and fly apart.

Page 17 Pressure-sensitive alarms can be fitted on window sills or behind doors. Other alarm designs use different switches, such as the gravity switch, which consists of a steel ball in a closed tube with two bare wires at one end. When the object is tipped, the ball rolls down the tube and closes the circuit between the wires, setting off the alarm.

Pages 22-23 This is only a scientifically fair test of conductivity if the amount of material is the same in each test. If there is more of one material than another of equal conductivity, it will seem to be a poorer conductor.

Page 25 The further along the coil that the bare wire touches, the greater the resistance to the current, and the dimmer the light from the bulb.

Pages 30-31 The more washing soda that is added to the water, the brighter the bulb shines until it is as bright (or almost as bright) as the test circuit.

Page 33 The object begins to become coated with red-brown copper metal. Depending on many factors, including the voltage of the battery and the purity of the copper, the object may take several days to become completely coated. During that time, the piece of copper will become thinner as it dissolves.

Pages 34-35 The higher the voltage, the greater the effect of the electromagnetism, and the bigger the movement of the pointer. A bulb added to the circuit will light when the current passes. The greater the voltage, the brighter the bulb will shine.

Pages 38-39 As the magnet moves through the coil, a current is induced in the wire and creates a magnetic field around it. This attracts the compass needle. Reversing the poles of the magnet makes the needle move in the opposite direction. Increasing the number of turns on the coil, or the speed of moving the magnet through it, increases the effect on the compass needle.

Page 41 Some domestic appliances will use more electricity per kilowatt hour than others. The ones suggested on the project all use more electricity than a television or personal computer.

Page 43 The thicker the wire, the higher its resistance and the greater the current it can carry without melting, or 'blowing'.

Page 45 When you cover the LDR with a hand, the LDR's resistance increases. This reduces the current and the bulb goes out. An LDR can be used in a circuit to switch on a street light when it gets dark, or to set off an alarm when a burglar interrupts a light beam.

When the temperature of the thermistor increases, its resistance falls. This causes an increased current and the bulb lights. A thermistor can be used to switch a refrigerator on and off.

INDEX